well-maintained sculpture park in a good location can enhance tourism, civic pride and a city's image; businesses looking to relocate, for instance, often factor in an area's cultural resources and recreational amenities when considering a move. Sculpture parks work double duty on this count.

Medallion awarded to Windsor,

recognized by The Canadian

Sculpture Society as the Sculpture

Capital of Canada.

Sculpture

By the River

a museum
without walls

L. Odette with Windsor Parks Commissioner Lloyd Burridge

Published by
Parklane Productions Ltd., Toronto, Ontario, Canada

ISBN 0-9731100-0-7
First Edition

Acknowledgements
From How To Look At Sculpture, copyright © 1989 by David Finn, (p. 2-5). Published by Harry N. Abrams, Inc. New York. Used with Permission. All rights reserved.

Amherst Quarries • Canada Building Materials • Canadian Coast Guard • Fergusson Glass • TransCanada Pipe Lines • The Hon. Herb Gray MPP

Photo Credits
John Riccio - Anne p. 79 • Spike Bell - Fireworks p. 96-97 • Kevin Kavanaugh - Cover, p. 3, 19, 20, 21, 23, 25, 29, 32, 35, 37, 41, 43, 53, 54, 55, 61, 69, 77, • Lou-Anne Barnet - p. 28, 31, 33, 45, 47, 49, 56, 62, 63, 65, 73, 74, 76, 81, 94, 95

Printed and bound in Canada
by Friesens, Altona, Manitoba, Canada, R0G 0B0

Produced & Designed by
Schawk Tristar Graphics

Table of Contents

When you walk by an important

sculpture in a museum, in front of a building, in a city plaza, or in a sculpture park, you are passing something that can open your eyes and mind to a new world. If you give it only a quick glance you will surely miss the experience. But if you stop, look carefully, walk around the sculpture, and watch it change as you see it from different angles, you will be able to make some astonishing discoveries.

The first step in this adventure is to realize that a work of sculpture is quite a different reality from a painting. A sculpture exists in space like a human being, or like a mountain, tree, or cloud, and it needs to be approached as an area that must be explored in order to be fully appreciated. When you hike up a mountain you encounter something new and unexpected at each turn - rocks, trees, caves, clearings, views of the valley below. You are on an adventure full of surprising and exciting twists and turns that are challenging, intriguing, perhaps exalting, and each hike up the same mountain can bring new experiences. The same is true of climbing a tree. Every time you go up you may find branches you never noticed before, and as you move around you

Flying Men, Bronze, 8 ft. high, >
by Dame Elisabeth Frink

get a different feeling about the forms you come upon as well as about the landscape below. And when in an airplane you fly through clouds and see from above what you are used to seeing from below, you understand something about the sky you never knew before.

You can provide an experience of being with sculpture for several hours as one walks around the grounds. There is no better way to open the eyes and heart to the unique qualities of three-dimensional works of art.

The great contribution of these sculpture parks is that they provide scenery to accompany the sculptural forms of the exhibited works. For when one looks at sculpture one sees what is in the background as well as what is in the foreground. The eyes take in the whole scene, and the sculpture becomes part

of its background and the background part of the sculpture.

Something about a great work of sculpture draws the eye to details. One looks incredulously at the muscles, bones, fingernails, hair, facial features, creases of flesh, and folds of clothing in the sculptures, marveling at how precisely the sculptor has rendered them. The same care and sensitivity is evident in an abstract work by the way joints are made, and different materials combined. It is as if the key to greatness lies inch by inch in the handling of surfaces which can be appreciated to the fullest when one examines small areas of the work. Walking around the sculpture, with your eyes peeled for lights and shadows and forms of flesh and hair and cloth, all making abstract patterns of unspeakable beauty,

you are in effect touching all its parts with your eyes rather than with your hand. You have a sense of physical contact with the three-dimensional creation standing before you. When your eyes are doing the feeling, you have a very special kind of experience. It is not the touch of the material that provides the critical impression; it is as if your eyes have fingers that are able to explore the work from all sides.

As you become more and more involved with sculpture, you will find that it can appeal not only to the sense of sight but also to the sense of touch. That is especially true of what has been called "organic" sculpture, or sculpture that resembles the forms found in organic life, reminiscent of those found in humans and animals and in other forms of nature.

Those who have had an opportunity to run their fingers over the surfaces of a masterpiece of sculpture know what a rare thrill it is. Touching the works is often prohibited in public places, yet physical contact produces a powerful response to the work. This is because the art of making sculpture is a sensual form of creativity. It grows primarily out of the emotional relationship we have to the human figure - our own to begin with, and more importantly those of others who arouse in us the passions associated with physical love. When we touch what sculptors have created we get the feeling that we are experiencing the same intense emotion felt by the artists when creating their works. Our hands repeat the experiences they had, and we become lovers of form just as they were.

I must confess that I knew very little about sculpture or sculpture parks when I met with

Lou Odette in February 1997. I still don't but I love being part of the team.

As Mayor of the City I was obliged to listen to a unique benefactor present his case. It sounded too good to be true so the City Councilors and I said let's all approve it right now.

It wasn't long before I was completely hooked as was most of my Council. What a thrill to run down to the river to see each sculpture being placed. The children bring their parents and the parents bring their neighbours. We are now the envy of nearly every city in Canada and many in the U.S. When I travel to major functions I make sure to give my cohorts our sculpture books. The visitors from Toronto, Toledo, Columbus, Ohio, London, Hamilton, and Cleveland bring their snapshots home to spread the same message.

Windsor is very proud to have the highest number of auto workers in Canada. Many are of European descent where art is taught in the early grades and their parks are full of sculptures.

The former Mayor of Detroit, Dennis Archer, has met with me on several occasions to see how they could change their waterfront into a sculpture park like ours.

Thirty years ago the Windsor waterfront was a rundown collection of 3rd grade hotels, old abandoned warehouses and derelict railroad spurs. Since then every Windsor Mayor had the same platform and objective and that was to turn it into a park. It became a two mile long beautiful garden, full of flowers, new trees and Bermuda grass. It was already a godsend so imagine the joy when it was turned into a sculpture park.

Windsor proved an ideal location for an outdoor sculpture park. The beautiful two mile long riverfront was just sitting there in all its beauty waiting to be plucked. The majestic Detroit skyline was a powerful background for sculpture. It's hard to keep your eyes from the site when you can sit on a bench and watch commercial freighters from all over the world ply the busiest river in the world. In deep summer the big yachts from Detroit and the four Windsor based yacht clubs sneak up against the seawall to get some snapshots of the sculptures. In midweek there can be as many as 15 professional gardeners trimming trees and manicuring the grass on the 2 mile stretch of waterfront.

When night arrives it's like a Christmas tree. Every sculpture has its own lighting hidden underground. The huge General Motors world headquarters building across the river in Detroit comes alive and the real thrill is when the lights on the Ambassador Bridge click on it's 200 Hi Density lights. The big sign of Ambassador Bridge, 10 ft. high on the very top towers, is the grand finale.

The Windsor Symphony is a regular in their band shell in the Odette Park playing mostly Gershwin. Many of the local industries sponsor the symphonies in the park.

Our insurance appraisals show that some of our permanent sculptures have doubled in value. We were voted The Sculpture City of Canada by the Canada Sculpture Society made up of 150 members with one man and group shows across Canada.

The park and the sculptures is under the supervision of Lloyd Burridge, Parks Commissioner, and Don Sadler, Director of the park.

Mayor Michael D. Hurst

It is with great admiration, appreciation and pride that, on behalf of the University of Windsor,

I salute the tremendous achievement that is the Odette Sculpture Park in Windsor, Ontario. This magnificent collection mirrors the University's own special collection of more than 20 sculptures and 50 paintings which grace our campus and many of our classrooms, all of which have been donated by Mr. and Mrs. Lou Odette. The outdoor pieces are open to the public and surround one of our major landmarks, the Odette School of Business, and it's 2000 students.

This generosity and imagination has given Windsor and its University something unique and very special. The strong message is that art is a vital part of everyday life. On campus, the collection provides opportunities for students in all faculties, not just the Visual Arts School, to expand their horizons and to learn to appreciate many different ways of looking at the world. On the riverfront, the Sculpture Park extends this opportunity to citizens and visitors alike,

UNIVERSITY *of* WINDSOR

with a special flair for attracting and amazing children.

In this way, the Odette collections greatly enhance life in our community and complement the new Art Gallery of Windsor building on the Detroit River and the nearby gems of the Detroit Institute of Art and the spectacular collection at the Toledo museum. The foresight of the Odettes, coupled with the leadership of Windsor Mayor Michael Hurst and his council and of Lloyd Burridge and Don Sadler of the Parks and Recreation Office have contributed a great deal to this community, and our 12,000 students.

The Odette Sculpture Park is a major tourist attraction, as well, and it is really helping to put Windsor on the map. Our unique border city will never be the same and we, at the University, intend to grow with it. As someone who has lived in many cities in Canada, I have never seen such a unique combination of business savvy and artistic imagination – it is a dynamic duo!

Ross Paul, Ph.D.
President
The University of Windsor

Foreword

Lou Odette's association with the City of Windsor and in particular its art gallery is longstanding and significant. He and his brother Edmond supported the vision of the gallery's founding director Ken Saltmarche in moving the gallery from its original home at historic Willistead Manor to its central location on Riverside Drive. This new space, in a refurbished, former brewery warehouse, provided vastly increased exhibition, storage and work-space which regularly featured highlights from the Canadian historical collection. In 2001 when the Gallery moved into its new state-of-the-art home, Lou and Ed once again sponsored exhibition space in the building, plus an outdoor area to the west of the building for the display of sculpture.

Lou Odette has been a keen supporter of sculptors and their work for many years. His tireless efforts led to the establishment of Toronto's forward-looking *Sculpture Garden* in

1981. In 1997 he returned to Windsor with inspiring plans for a sculpture garden along Windsor's celebrated Riverside Drive. Today that garden, renamed the *Odette Sculpture Park,* provides the opportunity for many thousands of visitors who walk, skate and cycle the extensive riverfront parkland to enjoy, as it was meant to be seen. In 1998 The Canadian Sculpture Society recognized Windsor as the Sculpture Capital of Canada.

With the economic uncertainty and escalating costs of this last decade, the production of sculpture, one of the most costly art forms to realize, has been drastically curtailed in Canada. Unless specifically commissioned, most sculptors, particularly those working in traditional media such as marble, bronze or steel, seldom see their work through to completion.

With the support of the Odettes' numerous sculptors across Canada have been able to see their work come to fruition. Lou and his brother Ed, were awarded the Order of St. Michael's College, by the University of Toronto, for their contribution to the arts; and the Order of Canada for their lifelong contribution as humanists, philanthropists and patrons of the arts and education.

Glen Cumming
Director
Art Gallery of Windsor

Message From An Artist

by Ted Bieler

Sculpture is an awkward art form. Sculpture takes up real space and is often made of hard, heavy and obdurate materials. Some sculpture is abstract, some representational, some in-between. It confronts by its very existence.

Sculptors, and I am one, are dedicated to making sculpture. Making sculpture that has the physical presence and creative grace to get noticed in a public place is costly and often difficult. Who will support such an endeavour and in what public place will it be unveiled? With whom and with what information will this encounter with sculpture occur?

Lou Odette, already a long-time collector of sculpture, was first inspired in this direction when he created the Toronto Sculpture Garden in 1981. In this ongoing project sculptors are challenged to create work specifically for installation in this public place. Not only is a public, outdoor, urban, yet disarmingly intimate space provided, but through Lou Odette's funding, sculptors are given financial, technical, curatorial and publicity support to realize their proposals. The Toronto public, with the very best in contemporary sculpture placed before it is initiated in refuge, and by seductive confrontation, to make its acquaintance.

Under the supervision of its director, Rina Greer, 67 artists have created installa-

tions for the garden. The first 15 years of projects in this internationally renowned initiative, now in its 20th year, are documented in the Toronto Sculpture Garden book.

Sculpture is experienced bodily and is made physically using a range of traditional crafts and current technologies. Sculptors learn by making by hand, using all kinds of messy, space consuming and sometimes costly processes. Odette has had a palpable impact on sculptors in Canada by encouraging and enabling the education of sculptors.

He extended his support to emerging sculptors by creating a cast metals foundry and sculpture study center at York University and by support to other schools, including the sculpture foundry at O.C.A.D. He has made it possible for many sculpture students to use these enhanced facilities and realize their ideas through substantial scholarships and endowments.

The Windsor Sculpture Garden places sculpture permanently in a space that is a spectacular conjunction of the natural and the urban, the banks of the Detroit River in Windsor. Here notions of the contemporary and the urban recede in the presence of what can only be described as a mythic space, one of those gardens that has enchanted and changed our perceptions

since time immemorial. That space rubs off on the sculpture and, in turn, the sculpture encourages people to revisit the space and find new and renewed dimensions in it. Through sculpture visitors can enter the imaginative and mythic dimensions of this garden and are also reminded of the historical transformations of this landscape, once a wilderness, then the site of early human settlement and village life; with urbanization it was used by the railroads and most recently reclaimed as parkland by the City of Windsor, returning it to nature, to community, and to the creative imagination. Uniquely, the sculpture is also seen from the river by the many people traveling on one of the most heavily trafficked waterways in the world.

The sculpture is permanent; it is there to stay. Here in Windsor the sculptures themselves become part of the community, becoming familiar to those who use the space frequently; they are welcomed, tolerated, rejected, ignored, but there: obdurate, unmoving, rooted in place. Each sculpture proposes its own unique connection to its place and to those who encounter it there. Each sculpture in its stillness reflects and responds to the kaleidoscope of change in the river reflections, colour in the sky, the light and shade of the city skyline, the seasons of the trees.

My sculpture "Tower Song" is based on a small sculpture Mr. Odette had seen which provoked in him the idea of a sculpture tall enough to function as a sentinel. With the heavy boat traffic on the Detroit River, a vertical sculpture would mark the location of the Sculpture Garden from the river and the Detroit shoreline. The two-foot high model,

one casting, became 76 castings, each two and one half feet high bolted together internally to assemble the 25 foot high sculpture.

"Tower Song" takes its vertical stance from this impulse to mark and locate and, in an ascending spiral of movement, weaves through it the waves and ripples of the windy river. The river as axis of separation and shared connection is reflected in the symmetry and light bouncing off "Tower Song".

By creating a Sculpture Garden in Windsor, Lou Odette has offered the people of his home town a new way to celebrate their place. Celebration starts most naturally with children, children physically exploring, expressing, and proposing ideas through their very physical, active encounters with the world around them. Recognizing the natural affinity children of all ages have for sculpture, Odette has funded and promoted a program that brings school children to the park with their teachers for sometimes impromptu, sometimes guided tours. Later the children respond with short essays on their experience. It is a delightful, 'though sometimes sobering experience, to read these always enthusiastic epistles on encounters with sculpture.

The Windsor Sculpture Garden is the culmination of an idea started in response to sculpture. It is an idea about community building that recognizes one of the most ancient roles of sculpture, that of marking a unique place and providing a focus which anchors a common experience. Marking this place, the sculpture gathers threads of a landscape, a river, a history and a people, and offers them back for our celebration.

Now A Word About The Artists

You might not be aware that Canada is known around the world, not only for its hockey players, but for its sculptors. There are 150 members of the Canadian Sculptors Society and another 40 or 50 non-members. Most are University graduates in the visual arts and many are or were teachers and professors, some were practicing architects. Several have studied at the elite art colleges in the U.S., Canada and Europe.

They are not very busy doing commissions in Canada due to lack of interest by individuals and corporations, and through government cutbacks, but many are busy abroad working on commissions. This is Canada's loss, because you may never see the works of Edwina Sandys or Leo Mol. Anne Harris has commissions in Germany, Israel, South America, California, England and is in the prestigious Hirshhorn and the Albright Knox and the Smithsonian.

The late Bill McElcheran could not be with us opening day because he was in Italy opening shows in Venice and Rome. He has shown in Hong Kong, Tokyo, and New York. Gerald Gladstone has commissions in Los Angeles, Florida, London, England and Australia by their Capital Commission. Pauta Saila has been touted as one of the top stone carvers in the world. He is in

collections in most countries. His bio of shows is three pages long. Joe DeAngelis, Joe Rosenthal and Ian Lazarus say their future is offshore. Sorel Etrog and Hans Schleeh who are featured at the University of Windsor Campus are both in the famous sculpture garden at Storm King, New York. Steve Cruise is prolific and has a waiting list of new commissions.

Yolanda Vandergaast has her penguins in a prominent location on the Detroit River and Derrick Hudson has his three life-size bronze elephants up front in the park. Life-size Melancholy Baby in bronze is by Milton Hebald. He has his

main studio in Israel and another in New York. The opposite side of the Odette Business Building is home to nine more sculptures. Standing out is the lovers, made of pounded metal eight feet high by Hans Schleeh, called Embrace. He has been listed in many international art guides.

Exhibitions are planned by the Art Advisory Board, chaired by the Sculpture Park Director, Lloyd Burridge, and Vice President, Don Sadler. It is composed of artists, curators, architects and other arts professionals. The long list of volunteers on committees is shown on page 94 of this book.

Guitar Man, Bronze, 5 ft. 5 in. high,

AL GREEN

Al Green founded the Canadian Sculpture School
in 1967 and owned a foundry with Maryon Kantaroff.
He was a principal backer of the Sculpture Society
of Canada. See biography on page 93.

Trees, Four hammered brass trees, 4 ft. to 7 ft. 5 in. high

T

ONI PUTNAM

"Creation is mysterious" says Toni Putnam. Each one of these trees has been carefully cultivated. Using welding techniques which are uniquely her own, Putnam focuses intense heat as a force of uncontrollable change. In this heat each of the four trees "grows" in its own way. See biography section.

Space Plough II, Painted steel, 17 ft. wide x 8 ft. high

S OREL ETROG

Space Plough II asks the viewer to try and bring machinery into the museum, to see that even the most utilitarian objects of our creation also have at least some artistic and expressive component. Space Plough II has a strong but simple steel construction, a basic triangular shape and is painted in that recognizable cautionary orange of heavy duty industrial machinery. See biography section.

The King and Queen, Welded steel-painted, two pieces, 10 ft. high

SOREL ETROG

In many ways the addition of Sorel Etrog's The King & Queen into the Odette Sculpture Park marks a true moment of "coronation" for the Windsor City's waterfront collection. His sculpture probes the relationship between man and machinery.

STEPHEN CRUISE

Bell Measure MCMXCIX, 1999 7 ft. x 17 ft. >

Church bells rang for religious ceremonies and for important town meetings. Hand held school bells called children to classes or released them for recess. This hand held school teachers bell is reputed to be the worlds largest school bell.

The Measure of Cruise's title applies to the long wooden handle of the piece and references the image of a bar measure, a calibrated ruler used by archaeologists to take measurements of depth and range. The bell is aligned with the cardinal points of the compass. See biography section.

JOE ROSENTHAL

Consolation, Bronze, 5 ft. high >

In Joe Rosenthal's art the human figure is presented with impressive weight. The solid rounded shapes of Consolation display a substantial inner fortitude, what some critics have called his "enduring universal toughness." See biography section.

PAUTA SAILA

Dancing Bear, Bronze, 8 ft. high >

The massive artic polar bear, distilled to the base elements of its raw strength and intricate balance, is Pauta Saila's most recognizable subject. The shape of Dancing Bear represents one human imagination trying to understand or hold on to the incredible energy of the natural world. Dancing Bear has already become a beloved Windsor landmark, and one of the favourite stops on any walk through the garden. It was commissioned by the Odettes for the Park.

Cordella, Aluminum cast, 5 ft. high

MARYON KANTAROFF

"I think I was asking, where do we all come from?"

In Cordella we see Kantaroff's attention shifting to a universal fascination with the idea of origins. The piece is dynamic and seems to be growing organically. See biography section.

Rinterzo, Fountain and reflection pool, compressed granite, 10 ft. by 28 ft. long

Joseph DeAngelis

Titled with the Italian word for a billiard shot, and interactive in almost every element, Rinterzo invites the viewer to become a participant, to enter into a game which is simultaneously playful and sensual. Underwater lights and fountains make for night viewing.

E DWINA SANDYS

Eve's Apple, Welded painted steel, 12 ft. high >

This very feminine hand with its nail polished
fingertips is constructed out of three separately
cut planes of steel.

Eve's Apple captures that moment in the bibli-
cal story just after Eve has taken her important
bite from the fruit of knowledge. It is a complex turning point, an intersection at which
knowledge is achieved and innocence is lost.
The apple is displayed prominently, held
almost proudly in the fingertips, showing
off the marking of its bite. See biography
section.

Morning Flight, Painted steel, 20 ft. high

GERALD GLADSTONE

The geometric sculpture of Gerald Gladstone presents a striking model of interdependence. In *Morning Flight* we are presented with a complex balancing act. Think of the perfect v-formation of Canada geese in flight, or the balanced internal divisions inside every orange.

Chicken and Egg, Truck sprockets, Egg -white marble, 3 ft.6 in. long, 1 ft.6 in. diameter

MORTON KATZ

Morton Katz's whimsical Chicken and Egg. This sculpture presents children with a strange sort of feathered friend, built out of the odd but instantly recognizable medium of a gigantic chain from ready mix trucks. The chicken is juxtaposed with the solidity of its egg which is carved out of solid marble from Quebec.

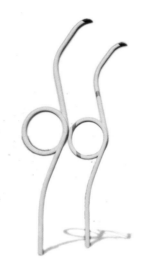

ANNE HARRIS

Tohawah, The only Canadian Swan, 38 ft. high >

In a very literal way, Anne Harris' sculpture represents a "fusion" of untamed strength and precise elegance. Harris compliments the skill of her sculptor's vision with the industrial tools of blow torches, fork lifts, electric buffers and sand blasters. Tohawah is named with a Native language word for swans and was originally commissioned because Odette is the Swan in Swan Lake.

WILMER NADJIWON

Neish Do-Dem, or (two marks) 51 ft. high >

Reflects the art and legends of the Pacific Coast First Peoples. Each totem pole presents brightly coloured story images and designs from the West Coast. Soaring 51 ft. high over the Detroit River is Thunderbird, topping the pole of the eastern side of sculpture.

HAROLD RICE

Images descend from Thunderbird and encircle the pole. Bear and Bear Mother. Images which represent more than an animal, introduce an important semi-divinity in the native legends. Neish Do-Dem show Bear with snout, teeth, eyebrows and paws. There is also a Bear sitting upright with a human-looking child in arms. See biography section.

TED BIELER

Tower Song, Cast Aluminum, 25 ft. high >

The spiral of life, found in plant, mineral and animal life, twists its way up Tower Song, suggesting potentially infinite progressions of form ascending upward, descending into the ground below or branching out from it.

The sculptor's fascination with ancient monuments, those of the Mayan and the Incas in particular, highlights the art of marking a place by delineating a point of view, a view that here embraces the free flow of a river at the crossing between two metropolises. He used 38 separate and different castings for Tower Song.

Audio Corridor, Stainless steel, 8 ft. x 22 ft. long

IAN LAZARUS

The sculpture deals with a lyrical phrasing of space, inviting the viewer to move through it as one would move through music if it could be made visible.

It is a favourite of the children who love to take a pencil and pretend they are a xylophonist.

Craft, Aluminum, Wood, 20 ft. wide, 7 ft. high

BEN SMIT

Craft, the piece currently donated to the Odette Sculpture Park by the artist is just coming off a critically acclaimed six-month exhibition in the Toronto Sculpture Garden.

It remembers a simpler period of North American history, a more innocent, probably more naïve time, when a flying saucer could activate feelings of curiosity, terror, humour and wonder all at the same time.

WILLIAM McELCHERAN

Business Man on a Horse, Bronze 9 ft. high >

In Business Man on a Horse, William McElcheran presents us with the now famous figure of his befuddled businessman awkwardly seated on his "trusted steed." The work seems to bring the viewer into a kind of shared compassionate joke. As many critics have noted however, McElcheran's subjects are not just the focus of his jokes, they are also under his protection. Encounter of two businessmen is on the front lawn of the Odette School of Business.

WILLIAM McELCHERAN

Encounter, Bronze, 8 ft. high   >

Bill is known worldwide for his Man on a Horse
and several versions of the befuddled businessman with his pork-pie hat. He has received
numerous awards and has had many one-man
shows in Europe. He was also well known as an
architect specializing in unique churches.

Embrace, Hammered Copper

Hans Schleeh

His pounded copper sheets end up as lifelike as a casting. His works are in most major Canadian collections and in public and private collections around the world. See his extensive biography.

Penguins, Aluminum, 48 in. high

YOLANDA VANDERGAAST

These three Emperor Penguins were cast in aluminum to Yolanda's 1 ft. high maquette. She painted the white bibs and yellow necks with iridescent automotive paints. Rumour has it that one of them was restless and went for a swim in the Detroit River and hasn't returned yet.

Melancholy Baby, Bronze, 6 ft. high

M ILTON HEBALD

Milton maintains studios in Rome and New York
and is represented by major galleries there.
Melancholy Baby was cast over 20 years ago
and has a Bavarian feel.

Mobile, Stainless Steel, 5 ft. x 5 ft.

Bruce Stillman

Bruce is a graduate of Northern Illinois and Minneapolis College of Art. His mobiles are engineering feats that keep moving long after a little shove. His bio reads like a party for the stars; Henry Mancini, Jaacov Agam, Robert Altman, Norman Ackberg. See biography section.

The Sisters, Sheet steel-painted, 9 ft. high

MORTON KATZ

Each sister in this black finished quarter is constructed out of the same essentialized steel template. Spiritual leadership is apparent in the strength of the Mother Superior figure which is located just slightly ahead of her community. The sculpture also serves as an important historic marker, honouring the long tradition of presence and personal strength displayed by the Ursuline Sisters who operated Glengarda School opposite the sculptures.

Amara, Bronze, 7 ft. high

SIRI HOLLANDER

Siri's first major bronze sculpture was Amara,
her horse as a child in Spain. She later moved to
New Mexico where abundant animals cavorted
by her house daily.

Circus Figure, Epoxy resin & fiberglass

DAVID PELLETTIER

The Mime is epoxy fiberglass from his early period of acrobats and clowns. His agent Walter Moos introduced David to some of his contacts in Europe and New York; this enhanced David's studies at major art schools in Europe.

Farmer Seeding, Bronze, 5 ft. high

A LFRED LALIBERTÉ

Alfred Laliberté is a well-known figure in the Montreal art world having created some of their most beautiful monuments. His series of bronzes, crafts, customs and legends often depict long ago.

DERRICK STEPHAN HUDSON

Tembo, Bronze, Mother 10 ft. high x 16 ft., Babies 5 ft. high and 30 in. high

When one makes a mould for a horse, a lion, a dog or for most large castings, the surface or skin is flat. With a large elephant we encounter hundreds of skin indentations, some as great as an inch deep. To make the end result look alive you have to capture every change. It took MST

Bronze three months of casting before the major welding began. The threesome are a major attraction of children both sides of the River. While at the Toronto Zoo, Derrick spent free time sketching and photographing elephants and other wild life.

Dignatali, Bronze

Mario Negri

Mario was a writer for the Domus Review and a confrere of Alberto Giacometti.

Ferropeinture, Painting or sculpture or both

RENE BROCHARD

Painting, or sculpture or both? Friend of Oscar Neimeyer, the renowned architect who persuaded Rene to promote "Ferropeinture,". Bernard Kisiel of Montreal introduced Rene to Dr. Stern, the Dean of Canadian Art Dealers.

NEIL COX

Tecumseh, Black walnut, 4 ft. diameter, 8 ft. high, 1,500 lbs. >

The name echoes down the corridors of history - as well it might. Of all the great native leaders on both sides of the Canada-U.S. border, he is without doubt the greatest. A master strategist, his handling of his native followers helped General Isaac Brock capture Detroit in the summer of 1812. A brilliant orator, he could bring tears to the eyes of white men. For more information see his biography.

I AN LAZARUS

Consophia, Welded metal pipe, 38 ft. high >

Two Iridescent steel triangles joined by a swinging boom, engraved with Inuit message. Ian spent most of his learning years at Pietrasanta in Italy as a stone carver. The Odettes were his major collectors over a twenty-year period. See biography section.

TED BEILER

Japanese Wave, Bronze ∧

Winner of the Invitational Contest For the Canadian Embassy in Tokyo, Japan.

LOUIS ARCHAMBAULT

Fetiche, Bronze ∧

From the private collection of Dr. Stern of Dominion Galleries, Montreal. Louis is
in major collections in Canada and the National Art Gallery features several pieces.

Milton Sherril

Knowledge of man, Bronze ^

Ian Lazarus

Carved in Pietrasanta, Marble ^

HAYDN DAVIES

Space Composition, Welded Aluminum, >
Red Beams, 30 ft. high x 24 ft. x 14 ft.

Haydn Davies specializes in dramatic large outdoor sculptures in bronze, aluminum and steel. The 30 ft. high aluminum Space Composition commands a large presence in the heart of Windsor, just opposite the new Casino. Haydn has written numerous articles for art magazines, including "Bridges" for the Pratt Institute, New York. See biography section.

J OE ROSENTHAL

Neighbours, Bronze, 6 ft. high   >

Joe Rosenthal was born in Romania and
came to Canada in 1927. He has shown in
12 countries and won numerous awards.

A. DUQUETTE

The Columns >

The four entrance columns that stand at the eastern border of the Odette Sculpture Park serve an important double duty. Though they work on one level as an elegant but understated marker to welcome viewers, The Columns also provide the garden with a strong historical anchor and are recognizably patterned on the Ionic order of Greek architecture.

Torso, Bronze, 5 ft. high

Zoya Niedermann

Zoya studied at Ecole des Beaux Arts, Montreal, Concordia University and de Voss Norvege; and has studied or shown in fourteen cities offshore.

Union Six, Bronze, 7 ft. 6 in. x 6 ft. high on 5 ft. high miramichi pebble base

BRUCE WATSON

In Watson's fluid sculpture the viewer is presented with evolving forms through various stages of organic development. Watson places all his emphasis on the work itself. "You do these things and then let them speak for themselves," he says.

MATT BEASLEY *and* PAULETTE HUNT

Inukshuk, Large Amherstberg Granite Slabs   >
12 ft. high

This is an Inuit word meaning "thing that can act in the place of a human". They are used for indicating which direction to travel, to warn of dangerous places, for locating a food cache, as a shrine to a person or historic place, and to act as helpers when hunting caribou. They are a symbol of our Canadian heritage

Equus, Bronze, 5 ft. high

EDWINA SANDYS

Equus the horse has watched over the park at
the University of Windsor for the past nine years.

The Wing, Bar Aluminum, 10 ft. high, x 10 ft. flutes
Granite Base, 7 ft. x 4 ft.,
87 pieces of 2 in. x 4 in. x 10 ft.
aluminum extrusions

MORTON KATZ

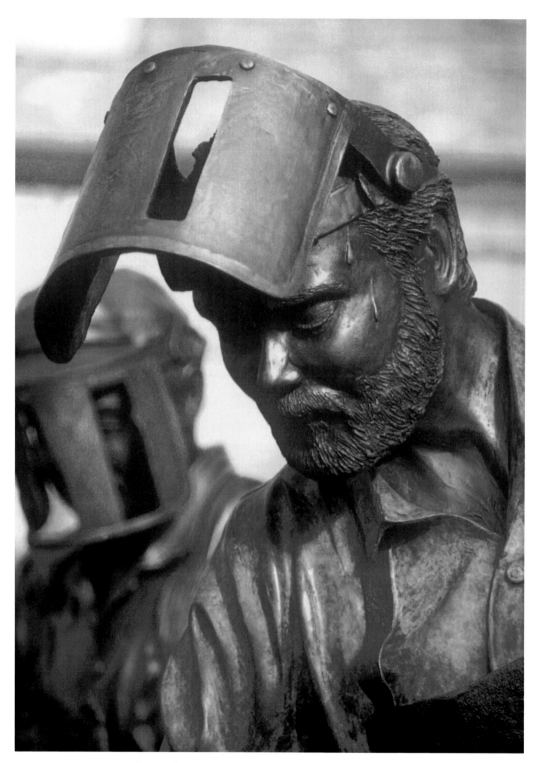

Four Generations, Bronze, 16 ft. high,

MARK WILLIAMS

Mark is a creative artist working in model construction at Ford Motor Company in Windsor and Detroit. His three bronze workers stand guard over the entrance to the massive motor plant.

Petro Kulyk, Bronze ∧

M. TRUTIAK

Tiger, Steel ∧

A. DUQUETTE

For My Love, Bronze ∧

B. ZORAN

Beatovic studied in Belgrade using brass, bronze and aluminum. The 6 ft. high *For My Love* has been in the Windsor Convention Centre for three years.

The Canadian Coast Guard donated the six ft. high steel ball, which is a damaged direction buoy from Sarnia.

L EO MOL

Anne, Bronze, 7 ft. high >

Leo Mol has studios in Winnipeg and the City
has built a large gallery in a forest to honour
him. He is also known as a master of stained
windows. He was a friend and creator for
Pope John Paul II, Dwight Eisenhower, John
Diefenbaker and a list of famous people.
See biography section.

Canadian Shield, 12 ft. x 16 ft. Aluminum nails, Sheet-aluminum, Plywood, Stainless-steel

DAVID PARTRIDGE

This is an outdoor project, so aluminum-clad panels and stainless steel are in order, also aluminum nails, to eliminate the problem of rust. Galvanized nails could have been used but aluminum's lightness made it more practical solution.

Homage to Louis, Bronze, 5 ft. high

SOREL ETROG

He commissioned this Homage to Louis 25 years ago to celebrate a wedding anniversary.

Artist Biographies

TONI PUTNAM

Toni Putnam was born in Boston and studied at the University of Rochester, l'Ecole des Beaux Arts in Fountainbleu, France and the Atlanta School of Art. In 1971 she co-founded the Tallix Art Foundry in Beacon, New York where she was a principal for fourteen years. During this time she explored and refined the innovative welding. She presented her work internationally in Tuscany, Italy and New Delhi, India. In 1996, Toni Putnam was elected as a Fellow of the National Sculpture Society of America.

SOREL ETROG

He has been prolific as a sculptor, a painter, an illustrator, a poet and a filmmaker. His work has been displayed around the world from Israel to Singapore, India to Switzerland. He has shown at Solomon R. Guggenheim Museum and the Museum of Modern Art in New York City, as well as the National Gallery of Canada, Ottawa and Le Musee des Beaux Arts de Montreal.

In 1988, he was commissioned to represent Canada with a sculpture for the Summer Olympic Games in Seoul, South Korea. In 1994, the Government of Canada donated the sculpture Songbird to Normandy, France, commemorating the 50th anniversary of the liberation by Canadian forces. He has collaborated with distinguished international literary figures Samuel Beckett, and Eugene Ionesco and also maintained a close working relationship with Canada's famed communication theorist Marshall McLuhan. In 1995 Etrog was named a Member of the Order of Canada and in 1996 was appointed Chevalier of Arts and Letters by the Government of France.

PAUTA SAILA

Pauta Saila was born in 1916 in a small camp on south Baffin Island in the Northwest Territories (NWT). In 1967 he was chosen to represent Canadian Inuit Sculpture at the International Sculpture Symposium. His work has been presented in hundreds of exhibitions and he is featured prominently in several important public and private collections. Pauta Saila continues to live and work in Cape Dorset, Baffin Island, Nunavut.

STEPHEN CRUISE

Stephen Cruise was born in Montreal in 1949, and lived for extended periods of time in Seoul, South Korea and Tokyo, Japan.

Cruise's sculpture has been exhibited across North America, including three recent appearances in the Bienal Barro de America in Caracas, Venezuela. The six pieces of his Spadina Ave. series Places in a Book, reinforces his interest in ideas of localized history. His sculpture is featured in the collections of the National Gallery of Ontario and the Canada Council Art Bank.

JOE ROSENTHAL

Joe Rosenthal was born in Romania and came to Canada in 1927. He has shown in Mexico, Cuba, England, Holland, France, Italy, Spain, Greece, Jordan, Israel and Egypt.

His awards include first prize in the National Open Sculpture Competition for the Dr. Sun Yat Sen Monument. Since 1957, his work has been exhibited throughout North America and Europe. His most recent award is The Rabin International Presentation Sculpture, Los Angeles, 1996. He is a member of the Royal Canadian Academy the Ontario Society of Artists and the Sculptor Society of Canada.

BRUCE WATSON — p.71

Bruce Watson was born in Guyana. He came to Canada in 1957 and entered the Ontario College of Art, graduating in 1961. His work has been recognized and supported by the Canada Council, and has been featured in the public collections of the Canadian Department of External Affairs and The City of Toronto Sculpture Garden.

MARYON KANTAROFF — p.28

One of Canada's most recognized sculptors, Maryon Kantaroff, was born in Toronto. She majored in art and archaeology at the University of Toronto. She was assistant curator at the Art Gallery of Ontario from 1957-1958 and then pursued post graduate studies in American ethnology at the British Museum in London and Reading University, the Sir John Cass College of Art and the renowned Chelsea College of Art.

Her private commissions include monumental works for the Canadian Embassies in Tokyo and Mexico City as well as several sculptures for courthouses, hospitals, and synagogues.

DAME ELISABETH FRINK — p.3

Dame Elisabeth Frink was born in Thurlow, Suffolk, England in 1930. From 1947-1949 she attended the Guilford School of Art and from 1949-1953 she studied under Bernard Meadows and Willi Soukop at the famous Chelsea School of Art. Solo exhibitions of her work has been stages in most of the world's finest galleries. Among her best know works are the Eagle Lectern in Coventry Cathedral, Man on a Horse in Piccadilly Circus and the Kennedy Memorial in Dallas, Texas.

Elisabeth Frink's honorary titles include honorary degrees from Oxford, Cambridge, the University of Surrey, University of Warwick, and University of Exeter. She was awarded a Doctorate by the Royal College of Art in1982. The British Postal Service released a commemorative stamp honouring her as one of the outstanding women of the 20th Century. Elisabeth Frink died in 1993. Mr. Odette visited Elizabeth at her estate in southern England.

EDWINA SANDYS — p.30

The artistic appeal of Edwina Sandys lies in her diverse subject matter which ranges from the lighthearted to the profound. Internationally renowned as a sculptor, British born, Edwina Sandys divided her working life between London and Tuscany, Italy before moving to New York City where she now lives. Her work has always reflected a strong social consciousness, focusing on several key issues of contemporary society; children, family, war and peace, women and the environment. Her monumental sculptures have been installed at United Nations centres in Geneva, Vienna, New York City and Rio de Janerio.

In 1990 her political and artistic passions were combined once again in a major piece entitled, *Breakthrough*, installed at Westminster College, Fulton, Missouri where, in 1946, Winston S. Churchill, Edwina's grandfather, made his famous "iron curtain" speech. *Breakthrough* is constructed from eight massive sections of the Berlin Wall.

JOSEPH DeANGELIS p.29

Joseph DeAngelis was born in Providence, Rhode Island in 1938. He has been a lecturer and professor in the School of Visual Arts at the University of Windsor. DeAngelis earned his Master of Fine Arts Degree from Syracuse University. In 1976 he was selected to participate in Spectrum Canada, as part of the Canadian art exhibition for the Montreal Olympic Games.

He has exhibited in numerous local exhibitions as well as shows in Toronto, Detroit, New York, Germany, Italy and Spain.

GERALD GLADSTONE p.32

Gerald Gladstone was born in Toronto, Ontario. He was resident sculptor at the Royal College of Art in London, England where he met Henry Moore who became his mentor and friend.

Gladstone's work has been exhibited in major galleries across North America and Europe. Some of his noteworthy commissions include the Martin Luther King, Jr. Memorial in Compton, California and three major works for Expo '67 in Montreal. He has been a lecturer at the University of Toronto.

His birds at the park are a favorite of children.

ANNE HARRIS p.34

Anne Harris was born in Woodstock, Ontario. She studied at Central Technical School and the Ontario College of Art. Her work has been featured in nearly 40 exhibitions across North America and is included in over 100 private and public collections. These include: the Albright Knox Gallery, the Canadiana National Capital Collection, Outdoor Sculpture at Rideau Hall (the official residence of the Governor General of Canada) and the Chongquing Fine Art Museum in China. Anne Harris has won Ontario Society of Artists awards on two occasions and exhibited her work throughout Canada, the United States and Europe.

MORTON KATZ p.33-50-75

Morton Katz began his career as an architect, and held a professorship at the University of Toronto, Faculty of Architecture for ten years. During that time, sculpture became a natural, creative extension to his profession. He has exhibited at major Toronto galleries including the John Black Aird Gallery, the Koffler Gallery and the Ontario Association of Architects Gallery.

His work is featured in private collections across the United States and Canada and has also appeared at the Art Dialogue Gallery in Buffalo, New York. Katz continues to work in the field of architecture while maintaining lecturing positions at the Avenue Art School, and the Art Centre at Central Technical School.

WILMER NADJIWON

Carver and Past Chief of The Chippewas of Nawash Wilmer Nadjiwon has spent many years travelling to Vancouver Island studying the art of the totem pole. He has exhibited his work in Canada, Europe and the United States.

A renowned carver, Wilmer Nadjiwon has one of his large carvings, Maturity Scene, on permanent display at the Canadian Embassy in Paris. Nadjiwon carves the animals of his area, turtles, beavers and owls as well as native dancers and warriors.

HAROLD RICE

Master Carver from British Columbia Harold Rice, a Coast Salish Status Indian. He studied carving with the renowned native master carver Norman John.

Recurring images and symbols in Rice's work include the salmon, the eagle, the raven, the bear, the wolf and the killer whale.

Rice's carvings have been exhibited in Toronto, at the McMichael Canadian Art Collection, The National Arts Centre and The Tandanya Aboriginal Art Institute. He was commissioned to carve a 20 foot canoe for Expo '98 in Portugal which is on permanent display at the Canadian Embassy in Lisbon.

TED BIELER

Ted Beiler, sculptor and Professor of Fine Art at York University, is the creator of many privately owned and public sculptures, amongst them, Triad on Front Street in Toronto, Tetra in Portsmouth Harbour, Kingston and Wave Breaking at the Canadian Embassy in Tokyo, Japan.

Born in Kingston, Bieler studied art at Cranbrook Academy of Art, in Detroit and has been teaching, exhibiting and making public sculpture since graduating. His interest in metal casting processes has led him to experiment with new technologies in his own sculpture and to work with Mr. L.L. Odette in establishing the complete foundry in the Odette Centre for Sculpture at York University.

IAN LAZARUS

Born in Toronto, Canada in 1951, Ian Lazarus started his sculpture career in 1972 as a stone carver. He spent 11 years travelling living and learning sculptural techniques in Mexico, California, Greece, Italy and Canada. As his sculptural language evolved, Lazarus moved from stone carving to incorporating a wider spectrum of materials and techniques into his creative endeavours.

Ian Lazarus has had more than 30 exhibitions since 1977 ranging from the Instituto Nacional de Belles Artes in Mexico, to The Sculpture Court in Harbourfront, Toronto. His work has been displayed in the National Gallery of Malaysia, Kuala Lumpur, the Art Gallery of Hamilton, the University of Moncton Gallery, New Brunswick, Butler House Gallery, Kilkenny, Ireland and the Japan International Contemporary Art Fair in Yokohama.

His 22 ft. high mammoth Pipe triangles can be seen from Detroit. They were commissioned by Odette. His collectors include the National Gallery of Malaysia, the Town of Freshford in Kilkenny

County, Ireland, and the University of Windsor.
He has received grants and awards from the Canada
Council, the Ontario Arts Council and the Ontario
Ministry of Citizenship, Culture and Recreation.

WILLIAM McELCHERAN p.42-44

William McElcheran was born in Hamilton, Ontario.
He graduated from the Ontario College of Art in
Toronto and was awarded the Lieutenant-Governor's
Medal. His famous businessmen with pork pie hats
are found in corporate collections all over the world.
He has produced public commissions in Canada,
the USA, Germany, Italy, and Japan. William
McElcheran was a member of the Royal Canadian
Academy. He died in February, 1999.
The Odette's were his largest collectors.

BEN SMIT p.41

Ben Smit was educated at the Ontario College of Art
(OCA) and earned his honours diploma in 1982.
During this time he also participated on OCA's Off
Campus Studio Program in New York City. For more
than a decade his sculpture has been prominently
featured in major group exhibitions throughout
the Toronto area. Ben Smit currently lives
and works in Toronto.

Craft, the piece currently donated to the Odette
Sculpture Park by the artist is just coming off a criti-
cally acclaimed six-month exhibition in the Toronto
Sculpture Garden.

It remembers a simpler period of North American
history, a more innocent, probably more naïve
time, when a flying saucer could activate feelings
of curiosity, terror, humour and wonder all at the
same time.

BRUCE STILLMAN p.49

Born in Minneapolis, Minnesota in 1958 he studied
at Northern Illinois University 1976-1977. In 1980
he attended the Minneapolis College of Art and Design
Extension and in 1984 the University of Minnesota
Extension.

SELECTED PRIVATE COLLECTIONS
Mr. & Mrs. Norman Ackerberg, Malibu, California.
Yaacov Agam, Paris. Robert Altman, Los Angeles,
California. Empress Fara Diba, Donald Harvie,
Calgary, Alberta, Canada. Henry Mancini, Vail,
Colorado. Sam Sachs, Detroit, Michigan. Mr. & Mrs.
Walter Walker, Minneapolis, Minnesota.

SELECTED CORPORATE COLLECTIONS
General Mills, Minneapolis, Minnesota. Dayton
Hudson Properties Minneapolis, Minnesota.
Mayo Clinic. Devonian Foundation, Calgary,
Alberta, Canada.

RENE BROCHARD p.57

Is it a painting or is it a steel? It's both. Mr. Brochard was living in France when he had an idea to blend the two.

In 1960 in Brazilia while doing murals in the University for the well-known architect Oscar Niemeyer, Brochard originated the idea of cutting and forging steel pieces as a third dimension to his paintings by creating real shadows, setting off a relief to project shapes or objects from his canvas.

St. Evremont viewed and appraised Brochard's work at the Romanet-Vercel Gallery in New York and assigned the term "Ferropeinture" to it. This gave an excellent idea of his new art form which Brochard initiated. Thus was born "the new school of metal." Mr. & Mrs. Odette bought his "Donkey Man" from Dominion Galleries, Montreal in 1978. It hangs in the main rotunda of the Odette School of Business at the University of Windsor. The hard cover book on Ferropeinture is a masterpiece of over 200 pages each and the book was hand produced with a limited edition of 1,250. 1,000 are numbered and signed by Rene Brochard. 250 copies are marked H.C. Many pages are removable limited editions in colour. The books are in real demand by artists who are painters and sculptors but none appear to have surfaced in Canada.

Mr. Bernard Kisiel his Design Manager is now retired and living in Montreal. His acquaintance with Brochard is mutual admiration for discovering this new technique.

His New Orleans series of jazz are lifelike with the horn in brass and the oil paintings in bright shades. He visited Japan, Mexico, Central America, Brazil, Israel and other countries selling his new ideas.

DAVID PELLETTIER p.52

Early on David Pellettier was spotted as a sensitive, unique artist. His first show in 1976 was a sellout and his clients are often repeaters who move in early to capture these limited editions. Presently he teaches art at his Alma Mater O.C.A.D. in Toronto and he served as the Chair of the Sculpture/Installation Program in the early 1990's.

He has participated in 36 exhibitions coast to coast since graduating from the Ontario College of Art in 1973. Twelve of these shows were solo. He was awarded a one year residency at Cite Internationale des Arts in Paris and has done research in France, Germany, Italy and England. The show, "Three Canadian Sculptors" travelled from University of London, England to Strathclyde University, Glasgow, then University of Sussex in Brighton to Bradford, then to Canadian Cultural Centre, Brussels, Belgium. He works in bronze and fiberglass. His porcelain works were exhibited in Badisches Landesmuseum, Karlsruhe and Museum der Deutschen Porzellanindustrie, Hohenberg/Eger and Stadtische Museem Heilbronn, Germany.

The Circus Figure is epoxy and fiberglass and is from his period of acrobats and clowns in very limited editions. They are in varied private and public gallery collections. Gallery owner Walter Moos who handled Pellettier's work during this period calls him Canada's most outstanding young artist with a high personal vision whose works give a timely and convincing message.

HANS SCHLEEH

Born in Koenigsfeld, in Germany's Black Forest in 1928, the sculptor studied at Lahr School for Sculptors with Richard Class and the Fine Arts Academy in Karlsruhe. He was commissioned to do sculptures for several churches, particularly the Ste. Anne de Beaupre, Basilica. His first break came in 1960 when Dr. Max Stern, owner of the Dominion Gallery in Montreal, sponsored a one-man show of his work. In 1961 Hans Schleeh held an exhibition at the new Art Centre Gallery, New York.

Many of his works were abstract or semi-abstract. In 1963-64 he returned to Europe to study in Switzerland, Italy and France. Most of his works are in museums and in private and public collections in Canada and the United States and around the world. Perhaps his work is most familiar to the people of Montreal, where his marble and metal sculptures are on permanent display in many public places. He also created a large piece for Expo 67, a marble statue of a man and woman. Hans Schleeh, died at the age 72 on July 16th, 2001.

COLLECTIONS
The collections with his work include those of the Vancouver Art Gallery, the Montreal Museum of Fine Art, Nathan Cummings Collection, Chicago. Mr. & Mrs. Charles Bronfman, Montreal. Mr. & Mrs. Mel Dobrin, Montreal, Mr. & Mrs. L. L. Odette, Toronto. Mr. A. J. Latner, Toronto. Mr. Lawrence Freeman, Ottawa. Mr. Walter Koerner, Vancouver. The Power Corporation, Montreal. Mr. & Mrs. Sam Zacks, Toronto. His work is also at the Tel Aviv Museum and the Bloomfield Collection in London.

MARIO NEGRI

MARIO NEGRI was born in Genoa in 1916, he attended his first school in that city and continued on to Milan. He carried to fulfillment the first biennale of the faculty of architecture and the Polytechnic. At the end of the war in 1945 he began a long period that intentionally meant hard professional training. From Milan artists he learnt the virtues of "trade" like the essentials in order to undertake the artistic jobs. He executed an innumerable series of jobs on a commission basis.

He also carried out the activity of critic of art for the Domus Review. He held his first personal show in Milan in 1957. The years of intense and formative human and cultural designs were met through Alberto Giacometti, Vittorio Serene, Russoli Franc, and photographer Ugo Mulas. Mario Negri died in Milan in 1987.

ZOYA NIEDERMANN

Zoya recent work establishes her as a mature sculptress.

She studied at Ecole des Beaux-Arts, Montreal, University Concordia, Montreal, Ecole des Beaux-Arts de Voss, Voss, Norvege.

She has shown at University of Concordia, Montreal, Dominion Gallery, Montreal, Studio d'art La Subbia, Livorno, Italy. Gallery Poma, Lugano, Switzerland. Biennale Fujisankei, Tokyo, Japan. Grand Palais FIAC, Paris, France. Art Chicago, Chicago, U.S. Art Frankfurt, Francfort, Allemagne. Art Miami, Miami Beach. U.S. Strasbourg, France.

She has created works for Harbourfront, Toronto and the Shaw Festival at Niagara-on-the-Lake.

YOLANDA VANDERGAAST

Yolanda VanderGaast is a graduate of the Ontario College of Art & Design and majored in mould making, casting wax and sand moulding, patinizing & enlargements. She taught art in a continuing education program for the York Board of Education. Commissions include:- Toronto Fire Services, Toronto, On. "The Last Alarm" Fallen Firefighter Memorial, Harbourfront Station #9. Odette Sculpture Park, Windsor, On. "Penguins on a Waterfall". Writers Guild of Canada, Annual Award design. Canadian Heart and Stroke Foundation, Award design.

Her three life-size Emperor Penguins on a hill at the Odette Sculpture Park was a hit with the children and the press. They both were concerned when someone "borrowed" one of the penguins and hasn't returned it yet.

LEO MOL

Leo Mol was born in Ukraine in 1915. He studied at the Leningrad Academy of Arts, and later continued his studies in Berlin and the Hague. In 1948 he and his wife, Margareth, came to Canada and made their home in Winnipeg. Mr. Mol is a sculptor of world renown and has carried out commissions of world figures such as Pope John Paul II, Dwight D. Eisenhower and John Diefenbaker. He is a member of the Royal

Canadian Academy and in 1989 was appointed an officer of the Order of Canada in recognition of his artistic contributions to his adopted country. The Leo Mol Sculpture Garden officially opened in Winnipeg's Assiniboine Park in 1992. Since that time, the garden has attracted visitors from around the world, and enriched the cultural life of Winnipeg.

NEIL Z. COX

Neil was born in Ingersoll, Ontario, in 1955 and had an interest in working with wood early in life. At the age of 26, he was making furniture in Vancouver, and a few years later began carving wood. Neil is essentially self-taught, having apprenticed with Stefan Vinyarszky in North Carolina, and spending six months in Italy learning to carve marble. He has traveled widely, visiting sculptors and museums throughout North America and Europe in order to expand his artistic knowledge and ability. He has won several Best of show awards at woodcarving shows across North America. His work is primarily figurative in style and often allegorical. He currently lives in Toronto.

TECUMSEH

Tecumseh was an honorable man at a time when honour was a scarce supply. His life goal of uniting the thousands of Natives People, against the settlers and the American government, took him on a journey from Wisconsin to Florida. Throughout his life Tecumseh remained a man of principle and courage. It is acknowledged that the Indians in Detroit, crossed the Detroit River at Sandwich on the site of the Odette

Sculpture Park. The town of Tecumseh in greater Windsor stands as a beacon to a rare Canadian leader. The miles of sandy beach and shallow waters were on his last retreat.

His last journey was from Amherstburg to Windsor, on to Tecumseh, then to Lake St. Clair, up the Thames River past Chatham to Moraviantown where he was killed and never found. The legend of the mighty man saved by his god lived on.

In the fall of 1998, carvers across Canada and the U.S. were notified of an open competition for a commission to be sculpted for The Windsor Wood Carving Museum. All entrees were numbered to eliminate any partiality and knowledge of the carver by the judges (who had carving and/or an art background). Neil Cox's sculpture was chosen by this panel.

The black walnut used, although not quite a 100 years old, ran three to four feet in diameter and eight feet tall, weighing approx. 1500 pounds. Neil's model was made from chicken wire, duct tape, and a blanket. The initial carving was worked with a chain saw. The statue weighs 800 pounds and stands seven feet tall. The sculpture of Tecumseh is presently housed at the Windsor Wood Carving Museum, in the cities Main Library.

Numerous books have been written on Tecumseh. For children we can recommend a soft cover, 63 pages, by Pierre Berton, "The Death of Tecumseh" published by McClelland & Stewart Inc. Toronto. Also available is a 450 page hard cover book, by author John Sugden, published by Henry Holt & Co, New York.

SIRI HOLLANDER p.51

Born in New York in 1959, Siri lived most of her childhood in Andalusia, Spain. Influenced by an artist family background, she began sculpting at the age of seventeen. After apprenticing with several accomplished sculptors both in America and Spain, she began her own work focusing equally on Steel and Bronze.

Horses and other animals were a natural direction for her work to follow. Surrounded by horses as a child and witnessing the fighting bulls of Spain gave her an instinct for the inherent drama of these animals.

Combining a special cement mixture with steel has allowed her the fluidity of metal with the timelessness of stone. This process enables her to capture the essence of the animal's nature. The characteristic rough texture and movement of line make Siri's work easily identifiable in both cement/steel and bronze.

Her work has been widely recognized and is included in many public, corporate, and private collections in America and Europe.

At age 9 in Spain she owned a horse named Amora.

DERRICK STEPHAN HUDSON p.54-55

Derrick Stephan Hudson was born in the United Kingdom. He earned a Bachelor of History degree before completing studies at the Ontario College of Art and Design. His work features wildlife forms in bronze, silver and stone. He has sculptures in private collections in Canada, the United States and the United Kingdom. Derrick Hudson focuses on wildlife art because he finds the animal form dynamic, diversified and tragically disappearing. "I hope to make people aware and concerned about animals in the wild and to assist in channelling this concern into greater animal protection

MILTON HEBALD p.48

Milton Hebald is one of the most important sculptors - many critics think the most important sculptor - working today with the human figure. When most other artists abandoned the human form to work abstractly, Hebald maintained his freshness and vitality in new statements of contemporary man. His unswerving faith in mankind is conveyed by the humor and passion he molds into his forms. Milton Hebald's work is represented in most major museums in the United States and a number in Europe, and is shown regularly in New York City.

MIODRAG BEATOVIC ZORAN p.77

Miodrag Beatovic Zoran was born in Belgrade, Yugoslavia in 1931. Although self-taught in sculpture, he studied art-casting design in Belgrade. He works primarily in bronze, brass and aluminum, but has also worked in such mediums as glass, stone and wood. His pieces celebrate a wide range of colors, and he prefers a weathered/matte look to the patinas that he uses.

M. B. Zoran is a member of Sculptor's Society of Canada and also a member of the Serbian Heritage Academy and Singidunum.

HAYDN DAVIES p.64

Haydn is a graduate of the The Ontario College of Art; The University of Western Ontario, School of Business; The University of Toronto, Dept of Fine Arts. Visiting Artist, Center for the Arts, Vero Beach, Florida. He was elected to Membership, Royal Canadian Academy of Arts.

Shows at:

Galleria Internazionale d'Arte Moderna, Venice, Italy, Victoria & Albert Museum, London, England, Galleria Nazionale d'Arte Moderna e Contemporenea, Rome, Italy, Musees Royaux des Beaux-Arts de Belgique, Brussels, Belgium, National Museum of Wales, Cardiff, Wales, Art Museum of South-East Texas, Beaumond Texas, Boca Raton Museum, Florida, Outdoor Monuments at the Ontario Government, Windsor, Ont.; Burlington Art Centre, Burlington, Ont.; Bell Canada, Trinity Square, Toronto, Ont.

Articles :

Omaggio di Haydn Davies - Galleria Veneta, Italy, 'Bridges' - Pratt Institute Exhibition, 'Ontario Art on View', Paris/Brussels. Listed in 'Who's Who in American Art'

MARK WILLIAMS

Mark has 18 years experience as a Mold Maker, Foundry man, and Sculptor. He is the Artist in Residence for Ford Motor Co of Canada. He has produced small bronze awards a foot high for the United Way, and Safety Awards for several Canadian and U.S. Ford plants.

ALFRED LALIBERTÉ

Alfred Laliberté's best-known works are: The Fountain at Maisonneuve Market, Sir Wilfrid Laurier's Tomb and the statue of Curé LaBelle in Saint-Jerome as well as his memorial to the Patriots.

He studied art in Montreal and Paris. It was during his apprenticeship at the Beaux-arts in Paris that Laliberté discovered and developed his passion for allegorical sculpture. He taught at the Ecole des Beaux-arts for 35 years.

PAULETTE HUNT & MATT BEASLEY

Paulette Hunt and Matt Beasley built the Inukshuk that stands prominently in front of the Windsor City Hall. Pointing to the north with one extended arm, it indicates the direction of travel to find the true home of all Canadians, in the North. It had to be the right shape to act as a guide to the travelers on the route.

Inukshuk are raised: to celebrate a historical place, to mark a dangerous place and as navigational aids across the tundra. The rock came from the Amherst Quarry. The Inukshuk weighs in at over twenty-eight thousand pounds and stands about fourteen feet tall. If you look closely at the words you will see that they are arranged in the shape of an Inukshuk. It would never have been built without the generosity of the people and the companies that gave so willingly of their time and resources.

Paulette Hunt is a Windsor native. Matt Beasley was raised in North Bay, Ontario and is currently employed as a Fire Fighter with the City of Windsor.

AL GREEN

Al Green began sculpting at Central Technical School, Toronto, in 1966. He founded the Sculpture School in 1967 and a foundry with well-known artist Maryon Kantaroff in 1972.

Al Green has participated in several group shows. A one-man show was mounted at the Sculpture Society of Canada's King/York Gallery. His sculptures are included in several public collections and also the private collections of George Burns, USA; Senator David Kroll and Albert Latner.

He has two major pieces at the Windsor Airport and is featured in June Ardiel's book on sculpture in Toronto. His work was included in a 1978 exhibition tour of London, Brussels and Paris.

ODETTE SCULPTURE PARK

STEERING COMMITTEE	SITE SELECTION COMMITTEE
CAROLYN ROURKE, CO-CHAIR	CAROLYN ROURKE, CO-CHAIR
LLOYD BURRIDGE, CO-CHAIR	LLOYD BURRIDGE, CO-CHAIR
COUNCILLOR DONNA GAMBLE	ELIO DEL COL
JANET GRAYBIEL	JANET GRAYBIEL
PETER HENDRICK	MINA GROSSMAN-IANNI
NANCY NICHOLSON	PETER HENDRICK
TOM PORTER	JOHN HRENO
COUNCILLOR SHEILA WISDOM	VERONIKA MOGYORODY
	MARY-ANNE STEVENS

PATRONS

THE P & L ODETTE FOUNDATION AND PATRICIA AND LOU ODETTE

THE WINDSOR SCULPTURE GARDEN WAS FOUNDED IN OCTOBER 1997 AND RENAMED
THE ODETTE SCULPTURE PARK IN SEPTEMBER 2001

A view of the Detroit Skyline from the Windsor Waterfront Park, celebrating the two cities annual Freedom Day.

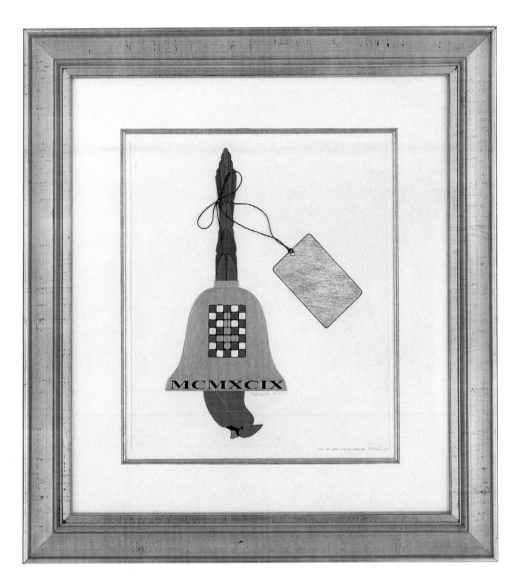

Bell Measure, Multimedia, 14 in. x 17 in.

STEPHEN CRUISE

Bell Measure resembles yet differs from *Bell Measure MCMXCIX, 1999,* the sculpture. The overhead view of the cardinal superimposed on the bell replicates a bell clapper and is linked visually with the bell handle. With elements that connect it to the bronze sculpture, it repeats the theme of time and tradition from a new visual perspective.

Salutation, Stainless Steel, 8 ft. x 8 ft. x 9 ft.

RALPH HICKS

Sculptor Ralph Hicks likes to create what he calls "figures with attitudes". In *Salutation*, the attitude is respectful courtesy. The simple cuboid, favoured by Hicks for its immediate and striking appearance, is the only shape required to give life to *Salutation's* purely positive greeting.

XIAOFENG YIN

Spiralling steel moving upward and outward, linking and joining two cultures and two countries is the creative force for *Ribbon of Friendship.* This painted steel sculpture winds and weaves, unfurling and undulating to illustrate the links of friendship between China and Canada. The piece is firmly grounded and appears balanced, featuring two red ribbons, which turn and twist towards the sky, seeking the future while resting on the present.

Ribbon of Friendship, Painted Steel, 11 ft. x 15 ft.

R ALPH IRELAND

This 2,000-pound relief, with its carved crew of twelve,
is a life-sized replica of the massive canoes that explored
the waters of Canada over two centuries ago, allowing
the young nation's vital fur trade to flourish. The opportunity to recreate a piece of our heritage with this piece
is very dear to the sculptor who laments, "Canada has got
a great, great history, and we forgot it."

Voyageur Canoe, Basswood, 26 ft. long x 5 ft. high

Ce relief de 2000 livres, avec son équipage de 12 personnages sculptés, est une réplique grandeur nature des rands canoës à bord desquels les explorateurs ont parcouru le Canada, il y plus de deux siècles, permettant au commerce des fourrures de faire vivre ce jeune pays. L'occasion de faire ainsi revivre une partie de notre histoire a été fort appréciée du sculpteur, qui ne peut s'empêcher de constater que "le Canada possède une très grande histoire, que nous avons pourtant oublié".

Le canoë des voyageurs, Tilleul, 26 pieds de long x 5 pieds de large

Composition with Five Elements, Painted aluminium, 7 ft. x 22 ft. x 8 ft.

HAYDN DAVIES

Composition with Five Elements demonstrates Haydn Davies' fascination with the irregular spaces created between large forms and the way in which they can "alter with even a slight change in viewpoint." As the viewer walks around the sculpture, simple shapes suspended in space will shrink, grow, metamorphose and vanish.

SIGMUND RESZETNIK

The tradition of obelisk building dates back to ancient times. Cultures from across the globe, including the Egyptians in the east and the Mayans and Incas in the west, created these enormous towers to provide protection from evil forces, or to mark time and space for future visitors.

This S-shaped contemporary *Obelisk* stands guard in the Detroit River, linking the river and the shore and highlighting Windsor's proximity to the United States. In the background, the world headquarters of General Motors.

Obelisk, Painted steel, 15 ft. tall x 5 ft. wide

RALPH HICKS

Ralph Hicks was born in London, England in 1941. He came to Toronto in 1967 and made his career in marketing. He developed an interest in sculpture while still a student, but didn't pursue it until much later. In 1996, he began sculpting very actively, working out of his specially built Mulmur Hills, Ontario studio.

XIAOFENG YIN

A prolific sculptor and academic, Xiaofeng Yin has exhibited extensively in China, Japan and South Korea. He has created sculptures in wood, bronze, and steel. He has won numerous awards in China for his pieces, and he has participated in sculpture exchanges with South Korea. A bronze work, Guards, *won the Gold Prize at the Exhibition of Asia and Pacific Area Culture Art in the United States. He is the author of various publications on Chinese sculpture and art.*

STEPHEN CRUISE

Biographical information on page 83.

RALPH IRELAND

Ralph Ireland creates his sculptures in Saint-Sauveur, Quebec, with the assistance of master carpenter Serge Charron. Over 1,500 of his works, with 280,000 reproductions, are displayed around the world. In addition to his large-scale works, like Voyageur Canoe, *Ireland is also internationally renowned for his life-like sculptures of various waterfowl.*

Ralph Ireland a créé cette sculpture à Saint-Sauveur, Québec, avec l'aide du maître-charpentier Serge Charron. Plus de 1 500 de ses œuvres, reproduites à plus de 280 000 exemplaires, sont exposées à travers le monde. En plus d'être reconnu pour ses œuvres de grande taille, comme le "canoë des voyageurs", Ralph Ireland est également connu à travers le monde pour ses sculptures d'oiseaux et de canards.

HAYDN DAVIES

Biographical information on page 64.

SIGMUND RESZETNIK

A noted Toronto architect, Sigmund Reszetnik began sculpting later in life.

Photo Credits
Paul Drouillard - *Bell Measure* • Lou-Ann Barnett - *Salutation* and *Obelisk* • Kevin Kavanaugh - *Composition with Five Elements, Voyageur Canoe* and *Ribbon of Friendship.*